About this book

The giraffe is one of the most distinctive animals in the world, with its long neck and richly patterned coat. Although you could easily recognize a giraffe, do you know how it lives? How does a giraffe sleep? What is its nearest living relative? Why do zebras and other animals seek out the company of giraffes on the African plains? What is a giraffe nursery? How do giraffes fight? Cathy Kilpatrick, who has studied giraffes in Africa, provides answers to these intriguing questions and introduces us to the less well-known facts about these tallest of land animals.

About the author

Cathy Kilpatrick is a zoologist and a freelance writer and broadcaster. Her travels have taken her to Australia to study locusts and to many areas of Europe, Japan and Africa – where she studied giraffes in the Kruger National Park. In 1978 she and her husband were chosen by the BBC to make a film about the wildlife of north Queensland as an entry for the Mike Burke Award. She has written many books on zoology, including several for children, and is the compiler of "Two by Two", a radio quiz program about animals.

Sir Maurice Yonge, Consultant Editor to the series, is Honorary Fellow in Zoology in the University of Edinburgh.

Animals of the World

First published in 1980 by
Wayland Publishers Limited
49 Lansdowne Place, Hove
East Sussex, BN3 1HF, England

Typesetting in the U.K. by Granada Graphics
Printed in Italy by G. Canale & C. S.p.A., Turin

First published in the United States of America by
Raintree Publishers Limited, 1980

Library of Congress Cataloging in Publication Data

Kilpatrick, Cathy.
  Giraffes.

  (Animals of the World)
  Includes index.
  SUMMARY: Introduces the characteristics, habits, and
environment of giraffes.
    1. Giraffes—Juvenile literature. [1. Giraffes]
I. Title.   II. Series.
QL737.U56K54   599'.7357   79-18959
ISBN 0-8172-1086-5 lib. bdg.

Animals of the World
Consultant Editor: Sir Maurice Yonge CBE FRS

Giraffes

Cathy Kilpatrick

RAINTREE CHILDRENS BOOKS
Milwaukee • Toronto • Melbourne • London

Do you know how many bones support the neck of the giraffe? There are just seven. Can you guess how many bones there are in your neck? There are exactly the same number. Most mammals, in fact, have seven neck bones. Of course, the neck bones of the giraffe are huge compared to ours!

Because of its long neck, the giraffe is the tallest of all land animals. The record height for a giraffe is 6 m. (20 ft.). This is a little taller than a double-decker bus. The average male giraffe is about 5 m. (16 ft.) tall. He is called a bull. The female is called a cow. She is shorter and lighter in build.

The giraffe lives on the continent of Africa, from the land south of the Sahara Desert to the Cape of South Africa. At one time, millions of years ago, it seems that giraffes lived in Europe and Asia, for their fossilized bones have been found in these places. But today they are only found in Africa.

This giraffe is seen with Mount Kiliman-
jaro, in Tanzania, in the background.
Giraffes are found in their greatest numbers
on grassy plains where there are scattered
tall trees. This is called open bush country.
They also live on the grasslands – called
savannas – where there are few trees. Some
live at the edge of forests.

There is only one species of giraffe, although zoologists who study them recognize many different races – perhaps as many as thirteen. Facing p. 1 is a reticulated giraffe. Without doubt this is the most handsome member of the species. It lives in the open bush country of Ethiopia, Kenya and Somalia. The richly patterned coat is

made up of large, almost rectangular, dark brown blotches separated by a network of fine white lines.

This is a Masai giraffe, with blotches of brown covering its body. Masai giraffes live in East Africa.

The giraffe's only relative is the okapi (*right*), which also lives in Africa. However,

it does not live with the giraffe and it does
not look very much like its tall relative. Oka-
pis, which live in the tropical rain forests of
Central Africa, are deep brown and velvety
and about the size of a donkey. The okapi's
coat is always glossy and sleek, for it spends

a good deal of its time grooming itself with its long tongue. This tongue is so long that it can wash and clean the eyes, as well as reach the tip of its ears.

The okapi's thighs, haunches, tail and the upper part of its forelegs have black and white stripes. This is for camouflage. In the dappled light beneath the trees of the rain forest, the stripes break up the okapi's outline and help hide its presence from its main enemy – the leopard.

Unlike the giraffe, the okapi cannot see very well so it relies mostly on hearing, using its very large ears and its good sense of smell for protection from enemies. It seems to live mainly by itself, or with its young. If it lived in groups it would be more noticeable to hunting leopards.

The patterns on the giraffe's body are very attractive, but for the giraffe, as for the okapi, they are not decorative – they are a very important method of camouflage. When a giraffe is standing against bushes or among tall trees, the shadows and shafts of light blend with the patterns on its body. From a distance, the giraffe is almost invisible, as you can see in the next picture.

10

The giraffe's large head, held high by the strong neck, tapers to soft, hairy, mobile lips. Inside the mouth there is a very long tongue. The nostrils are two slits which can be opened and closed so that sand, fine dirt, thorns and leaves can be kept out when necessary. Each ear can be moved by itself and can pick up any sounds of approaching danger.

The large expressive eyes are the most important sense organ of the giraffe. They give it wonderful vision. A giraffe is a living lookout post and warning system. With the eyes placed so high above the ground, the animal can survey the landscape all around. It is the first animal on the African grass-lands to see an enemy, or any other possible danger.

This is why the giraffe is often found in the company of other animals. Zebras will crop the grass close to giraffes, for the giraffes will warn them if an enemy, such as a lion or cheetah, is coming.

Giraffes also gather together in small groups, with each animal facing a slightly different direction. In this way there is hardly a patch of ground that is not being

watched for enemies. This means that the zebras, like those here, can relax.

Antelopes also stay by the giraffes for their protection. Impalas are seen here with a giraffe. They are small, graceful antelopes that live in East and South Africa.

If you look closely at a giraffe in the wild you might find a small bird hopping around on its body. This is an oxpecker. It searches the skin of a giraffe for ticks, fleas and other insect pests. The oxpecker eats them. This bird's other common name is the tick bird. Sometimes it will even clean out the ears of a giraffe. Oxpeckers are useful to giraffes not only because they eat ticks and pests. In the process of feeding they remove dirt and bits of dry skin. If the giraffe has open sores, tick birds have been seen pecking at these wounds and aggravating them. However, the birds may be of use here too, for they may be removing maggots from the sore area.

Because of its size and efficient warning system the giraffe has few enemies. The lion and humans are really the only killers of adult giraffes. Sometimes several lions will combine to attack and kill an adult giraffe. Even this is rare. The lions usually choose the moment when the animal stoops to feed from a low bush or to drink water. In this position the giraffe cannot see the approach of the lions. The lions attack the neck and muzzle first. When it pounces, the weight of a lion is often enough to knock the giraffe

over. Sprawling on the ground, the giraffe is helpless. The lions kill it quickly. They break its neck or strangle it with powerful jaws. Then they can eat it at leisure.

The baby giraffe is in great danger when left alone by its mother. Even when left for a short period there is time for a hyena, hunting dog, lion, cheetah or leopard to kill it. Usually, however, the adult giraffes will see or smell an enemy. The giraffes defend the baby by kicking the attacker with their powerful long

17

18

legs and heavy hoofs.

Many giraffes, of course, die from natural causes or accidents. Even then, the body of the giraffe is soon found. It is a good source of food for many animals, such as vultures or small carnivores that live as scavengers. Here (*left*) a giraffe has died after getting itself trapped among the roots of a tree. A silver-backed jackal has found it and is starting to eat it. More than half of all giraffes born do not survive their first year of life.

Because giraffes are so tall, they can feed from the tops of trees and can reach leaves and twigs that few other animals can get at. Their favorite foods are the leaves, twigs and thorns of acacia trees, which are common in the African bush. The two giraffes here are feeding on acacia. Feeding like this, on vegetation above the level of the ground, is called browsing.

When browsing, the giraffe's tongue curls itself around twigs and branches. The tongue is extremely long. The giraffe can put its tongue out about 40 cm. (16 in.). The flexible lips tear off the twigs, leaves, shoots and fruit with ease. You can see (*overleaf*) how the giraffe does not seem to mind the sharp thorns that grow on the acacia tree.

The giraffe is a ruminant. This means it chews the cud like a cow, sheep or antelope. The food taken by the giraffe is quickly swallowed before it is thoroughly chewed. The giraffe has a stomach with four parts. The food first enters the paunch or rumen. Then it passes to the second part of the stomach known as the honeycomb or reticulum. Later, when the giraffe has taken in as much food as it requires, it finds a safe

spot where it can keep watch for any danger. Then it brings back the food from the honeycomb up its long neck into its mouth.

If you have the chance to watch giraffes in a zoo, safari park or in the wild, you may see them chewing the cud. Big lumps the size of a tennis ball can be seen moving up the giraffe's neck. In the mouth the giraffe mashes the vegetation down with its powerful grinding cheek teeth. It chews each ball of food for about 30 to 45 seconds, making a large number of mouth movements. In the photograph (*above*) you can see a giraffe chewing its food.

When the food is a thin, pulpy mush the giraffe swallows it again. This time it enters the third part of the stomach called the omasum. The last part of the stomach it passes to is known as the rennet-bag, or abomasum. This is most like the stomach of other mammals, including our own. Digestive juices secreted here are mixed with the food.

The only animal that can reach higher than the giraffe for twigs and leaves is a large adult elephant stretching its long trunk out to the full. The giraffe's other competitor for food is the long-necked, graceful gerenuk (*right*). This is a species of African antelope. It is less than 1 m. (3 ft.) in height at the shoulder when it is standing normally on all four legs. However, it can rear up and balance on its hind legs. Now it can reach almost twice as high and so can find the leaves the young giraffes feed on. The gerenuk usually uses its front legs to rest against the branches of the tree or bush so that it does not fall over while feeding in this position.

Giraffes can go for long periods without water. However, when it is available, they

drink regularly. They usually drink in the cool of the late afternoon or around dawn, and also after dark. Quite often there will be other animals at the water hole. Here a hippopotamus and an elephant are already drinking as the giraffe comes down to the water (*left*).

When it wants to drink, the giraffe cannot reach the water just by bending its neck. It must open its front legs and stretch them outwards at a very wide angle. Only then can

it get its head down to the water. It looks very clumsy and ungainly in this position. The single giraffe drinking in the picture on the right has straddled its legs and then bent them slightly at the "wrists".

In the picture above, one giraffe has its forelegs bent. The middle giraffe has opened its legs extremely wide without bending them. The third giraffe is keeping watch. When a giraffe is drinking it is an easy victim for a lion, so one giraffe is always on watch. Giraffes often drink without a pause for as long as one minute. Then they straighten up again.

As well as needing water and vegetation to keep healthy, giraffes need many minerals. They find salt licks that supply them with vital minerals to keep their bones and bodies strong and healthy. The salty soil mixture contains soda ash, sodium chloride (salt), bicarbonate and soda, as well as sodium fluoride. They not only lick the salt soil, they take up large amounts of it with their soft lips and swallow it. They spend quite a long time at salt licks (*previous page* and *above*). Other animals also visit salt licks, including antelopes, gnus and ostriches.

Watching a giraffe move is very interesting. When it is walking in a normal manner it uses a kind of movement called "pacing." Here both the front and hind limbs on the same side of the body move together. The front leg and hind leg on the other side then follow. The hoofs of one side are off the ground together. As soon as these two legs are put down, those of the other side are raised. The giraffe has a rather stately air when pacing, with its slow and measured movements. These two young giraffes following their mother are pacing.

When the giraffe is alarmed or upset it will change from pacing to a canter and then to a kind of gallop. Then the hind legs move together and the front legs move together. The neck sways back and forth rhythmically. When traveling fast the tail twists up over the back. Perhaps this is to keep the tail out of the way of the legs. The giraffe can run at speeds of more than 50 kph (30 mph) when it needs to escape from danger.

A contest between two bull giraffes is a spectacular sight. They do not use their

hoofs or legs to kick one another. They fight with their long necks and heads. Two rivals take up positions side by side or facing one another. They hold their heads high in a threatening gesture. Then one bull bends his neck outwards and swings back. His head or neck smashes against the rival's neck or shoulder. This behavior is often called "necking." The thud is fairly loud. The noise can be heard some distance away. Each battle can last up to twenty minutes. It then seems to fade out, with one bull just cantering or even walking away.

It is still a mystery why the males battle. There is not usually any female in sight, so it is not for her favors. There is no visible winner, although it is probably the "winning" bull that stays his ground and the "loser" that moves away. Bulls do not appear to hold territory, so the fight is not about the possession of a particular patch of grassland. The horns are not used very much in many of the battles but the hair does get worn away. Sometimes gashes and bleeding occur if a fight is very violent. The fights rarely end in the death of one of the contestants. However, one giraffe, the victim of a "neck-

ing" session in South Africa's Kruger National park, was killed. His opponent made a large hole in his neck just behind one ear. The top neck bone was splintered by a blow. Part of the splinter pierced the spinal cord.

A female giraffe is ready to have young when she is five years old. Her calf is born after developing in her womb for about fifteen months. The birth of a giraffe has been observed in captivity several times, but only on one or two occasions in the wild.

The calf's forefeet are the first to be pushed through the birth opening between the hind legs. The head is next, as it lies

close along the legs. The mother stands up for the birth so the baby giraffe starts its life with a sudden drop from about 2 m. (6.5 ft.). However, it survives this without injury. The protective membrane that surrounds the calf in the womb is usually torn in the birth process. Afterwards the mother sometimes eats this membrane.

The newborn animal rests for a while before attempting to stand up. This may be as long as thirty minutes to an hour after birth. It is a bit shaky at first, but it instinctively knows that it must get up. It will be safer as soon as it can move. The mother usually begins to lick her offspring as it stands. The newborn giraffe is about 2 m. (6.5 ft.) tall.

The calf also knows where to find its mother's milk. It nudges around until it finds the teats on her lower belly, hidden between her back legs. Sometimes the mother will nudge her calf in the right direction if it is going the wrong way. The calf will begin to suckle about one-and-a-half hours after birth.

This young giraffe (*left*) is practicing walking, only an hour after being born. Although most of the time it stays close to

its mother, it will venture some distance from her. This is because, with its excellent vision, it is still able to see the mother. A baby rhinoceros, on the other hand, will never stray very far from its mother, for it is very shortsighted and relies on its sense of smell for protection.

As the young calf grows, the mother allows other cows to approach and touch her baby. They will often groom the calf too. In the first six weeks of its life the baby giraffe remains fairly close to its mother. After this

it tends to stray away and explore for itself. By this time it is nibbling tender leaves, although it suckles from its mother for nine or ten months. All the time it is growing rapidly. In fact, young giraffes grow 0.3 cm. (⅛th in.) each day. This is about 1 m. (3 ft.) in its first year. It grows until it is about seven years old.

A striking feature of giraffe behavior is the "nursery" group that they form. The calves gather together and are watched over by one or more adult females.

These are called "aunts." The other adult
female giraffes can then go off to feed. They
can still see the nursery groups with their
good eyesight and can find them again
quite easily later.

The adult male giraffe, or bull, lives by
himself most of his life. He strides steadily
along, stopping only to feed and drink. He is
usually on the lookout for a female who is
ready to mate. At other times he will spar

with another male. When the male does meet up with other giraffes he never stays long.

The female giraffes, or cows, live in social groups with their young. Usually the number in a herd is quite small – fewer than ten animals. Larger herds are sometimes seen made up of adult females, young bulls and cows and very young calves. Occasionally a bull is part of the herd, having joined it for a short time. Scientists have studied giraffe herds in the wild for long periods. They are still unable to say which adult is the leader. Sometimes it is one cow that leads the way to a new feeding area; at other times it is another cow, or even a visiting bull. Also, it is not possible to say which member of the herd is the "lookout" for the group. The giraffes seem to take turns in no particular order.

Until fairly recently it was not known what the giraffe does during the hours of darkness. Does it, for example, go to sleep as we do? During the day the giraffe does rest and even dozes for a few minutes. It does this standing up. Quietly and gently the giraffe relaxes the neck until it droops downwards. Its eyelids droop and the tail stops flicking. It sits down only very rarely during the day.

If the giraffe does sleep at night, does it stand, sit or lie down? In the last few years scientists have been able to find answers to these questions. The giraffe does sleep at night and does so sitting or lying down. It sleeps by cat-napping—taking a few minutes' sleep and then waking up to check what is going on around it. It holds its head erect most of the time. When it wants to sleep more deeply it bends its head back beside its body. It can sleep deeply for one to twelve minutes, but usually it sleeps for only three or four minutes at a time. By dawn the giraffe will be on its feet again, probably feeding, and ready to start its new day.

Glossary

ACACIA   A thorny tree, common in Africa, which giraffes feed from.

CAMOUFLAGE   Concealment of an animal by its shape and color which blend with its background.

CRECHE   A nursery group in which young animals are looked after by a few adult animals.

DIGESTIVE JUICES   Liquids that help to break down food so that it can be absorbed by the body.

INSTINCT   A skill or ability which an animal has without being taught. For example, young birds are able to fly by instinct.

MINERAL   A solid substance found naturally in the earth.

OXPECKER   A bird that eats ticks, lice and other insects found on the skins of animals living on the African grasslands.

PREDATOR   An animal that hunts and eats other animals.

RACE   See SPECIES.

RUMINANT   An animal — such as the giraffe, cow, sheep and deer — which chews the cud.

SALT LICK   An area where MINERALS occur naturally at the surface of the earth.

SAVANNA   Flat, grassy plains.

SCAVENGER   An animal that feeds on the flesh of dead animals, especially those starting to decay.

SOCIAL   Living in groups.

SPECIES   A group of animals, or plants, which inter-
breed and closely resemble each other. Members
of a RACE belong to the same species but are
slightly different in appearance, because fitted for
life in a particular area.

TERRITORY   An area in which an animal feeds and
roams, and which it defends against others.

WRIST   The first joint in the giraffe's leg above
the hoof. Because the foot bone is very long, the
wrist is so high up the leg that it looks like a knee.

Further reading

Burton, Maurice and Burton, Robert, editors. *The New International Wildlife Encyclopedia*. 21 vols. Milwaukee: Purnell Reference Books, 1980.

Dagg, Anne Innis. *The Giraffe: Its Biology, Behavior and Ecology*. New York: Van Nostrand Reinhold, 1976.

Leslie-Melville, Betty and Leslie-Melville, Jock. *Raising Daisy Rothschild*. Simon and Schuster, 1977.

Mochi, Ugo and MacClintock, Dorcas. *A Natural History of Giraffes*. Scribner, 1973.

Spinage, Clive A. *Book of the Giraffe*. Houghton-Mifflin, 1968.

Picture acknowledgements

Picturepoint — London, 27; Natural History Photographic Agency, 16, 40, 41; Alan Hutchison Library, 35, 45. All other photographs from Bruce Coleman Limited, by the following photographers: Des Bartlett, 12, 30; Jen and Des Bartlett, 37; Rod Borland 29; Jane Burton, 3, 12, 14, 24, 25; R. I. M. Campbell, 4; Bruce Coleman 6; Gerald Cubitt, 31; L. R. Dawson, 20-21; A. J. Deane, 17; Francisco Erize, 28; James Hancock, 18, 46; M. P. Kahl, backcover, 36; Gareth Millard Jones, 8-9; Norman Myers, 5, 32-3, 34; G. D. Plage, frontcover, facing p.1; Masud Qurishi, endpapers, 23, 39, 42, 44; Simon Trevor, 2, 10, 48; Rod Williams, 19.

Index